# Béisbol! Latino Heroes of Major League Baseball

# FELIX Hernandez

## JOSH LEVENTHAL

**BLACK RABBIT BOOKS**

Bolt is published by Black Rabbit Books
P.O. Box 3263, Mankato, Minnesota, 56002.
www.blackrabbitbooks.com
Copyright © 2017 Black Rabbit Books

Design and Production by Michael Sellner
Photo Research by Rhonda Milbrett

Library of Congress Control Number: 2015954855

HC ISBN: 978-1-68072-047-1    PB ISBN: 978-1-68072-305-2

Printed in the United States at CG Book Printers,
North Mankato, Minnesota, 56003. PO #1797 4/16

Web addresses included in this book were working and appropriate at the time of publication. The publisher is not responsible for broken or changed links.

# Contents

# CHAPTER 1

# A Latino Legend

It's the ninth **inning**. No Tampa Bay batters have gotten a hit. Seattle pitcher Felix Hernandez hasn't **walked** anybody. His Mariners hold a 1–0 lead. There are two outs. The count is two balls and two strikes. Hernandez throws the pitch. Strike three!

## Superstar Pitcher

Hernandez is a powerful baseball player. He is known for his amazing pitching. In 2012, he pitched a perfect game against Tampa Bay. It was only the 23rd perfect game in Major League Baseball (MLB) history.

perfect game—when no one hits a pitched ball or is walked

# Fun Facts

right handed

WEIGHT

225 POUNDS
(102 kilograms)

6'

5'

4'

6 feet
3 inches
(1.9 m)
tall

**family calls him by his middle name—Abraham**

**makes about $25 million a year.**

1'

0

nickname is King Felix

# CHAPTER 2

# A Young Baseball Star

Hernandez was born April 8, 1986. He grew up in Venezuela. He was a star pitcher at a young age. By age 14, he could throw a ball 90 miles (145 kilometers) per hour. **Scouts** watched him play. When he was 16 years old, the Mariners signed him to a contract.

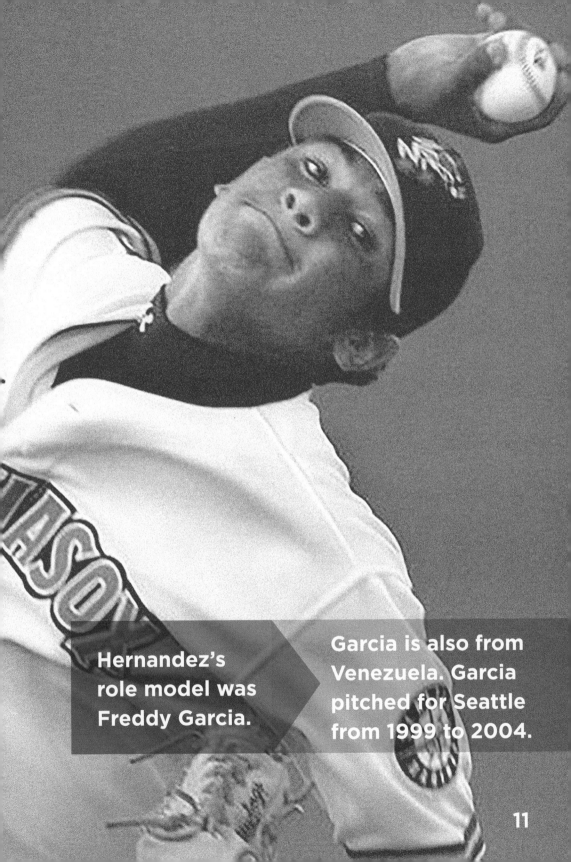

Hernandez's role model was Freddy Garcia.

Garcia is also from Venezuela. Garcia pitched for Seattle from 1999 to 2004.

# Number of
# Latino
# Major League
# Baseball
# Players

through 2015

642 Dominican Republic
341 Venezuela
253 Puerto Rico
193 Cuba
118 Mexico
55 Panama
17 Colombia
14 Curacao
14 Nicaragua
12 U.S. Virgin Islands
6 Bahamas
5 Aruba
4 Jamaica
3 Brazil
1 Belize
1 Honduras

## In the Minors

Hernandez came to the United States in 2003. He pitched in the **minor leagues**. In 2004, Hernandez **won** 14 games. He only **lost** four games. In 2005, he was named Pacific Coast League Pitcher of the Year. Hernandez was ready for the major leagues.

# CHAPTER 3

# In the

Hernandez pitched his first major league game August 4, 2005. In his second game, he didn't allow any runs to score. In the next game, Hernandez struck out 11 batters and won.

**Hernandez was 19 years old in his first MLB game.**

| 250 |
| 225 |
| 200 |
| 175 |
| 150 |
| 125 |

| 84.1 | 191.0 | 190.1 | 200.2 | 238.2 |
|------|-------|-------|-------|-------|
| 2005 | 2006  | 2007  | 2008  | 2009  |

## Getting Better and Better

Hernandez led all Seattle pitchers with 12 wins in 2006. He improved to 14 wins in 2007. Hernandez led the American League (AL) with 19 wins in 2009. That year, he pitched in his first All-Star Game. Hernandez was the youngest All-Star in 2009.

## Hernandez's Number of Innings Pitched

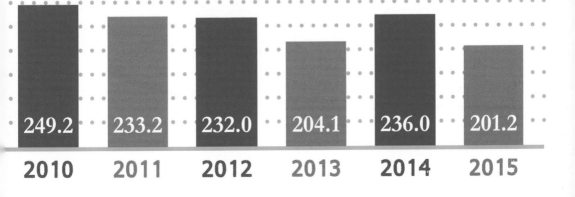

| 2010 | 2011 | 2012 | 2013 | 2014 | 2015 |
|------|------|------|------|------|------|
| 249.2 | 233.2 | 232.0 | 204.1 | 236.0 | 201.2 |

## One of the Best

In 2010, Hernandez won the Cy Young Award. The award is given to the best pitcher in each league. He struck out more than 200 batters. Hernandez also pitched more innings than anyone else in 2010.

**2014**

MLB Players Choice
AL Outstanding Pitcher

Big

Awards

2008

**Mariners MVP**

2010

**AL Cy Young Award**

## Perfection

On August 15, 2012, Hernandez pitched a perfect game. It was the first perfect game in team history. After the season, the Mariners re-signed him to a big contract.

| MOST Strikeouts by Pitchers from Venezuela (through 2015 season) | Felix Hernandez | Johan Santana |
|---|---|---|
| | **2,142** | **1,988** |

| Carlos Zambrano | Freddy Garcia | Wilson Alvarez |
|---|---|---|
| **1,637** | **1,621** | **1,330** |

# CHAPTER 4

# Continuing to Impress

Hernandez was an All-Star every year from 2011 to 2015. In 2014, he was the starting pitcher in the All-Star Game. He is the first Venezuelan pitcher to start an All-Star Game. In his career, he's made more than 2,100 strikeouts.

In 2011, Hernandez's fastball went about 93 miles (150 km) per hour.

## Games Pitched

| | | | | | |
|---|---|---|---|---|---|
| 2005 | **12** | 2009 | **34** | 2013 | **31** |
| 2006 | **31** | 2010 | **34** | 2014 | **34** |
| 2007 | **30** | 2011 | **33** | 2015 | **31** |
| 2008 | **31** | 2012 | **33** | | |

## Strikeouts

**77**
2005

**176**
2006

**165**
2007

**175**
2008

**217**
2009

**232**
2010

# Wins

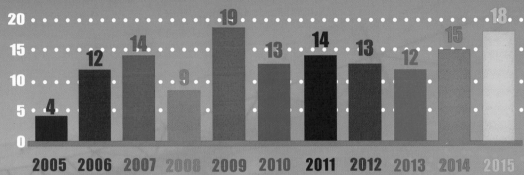

| 2005 | 2006 | 2007 | 2008 | 2009 | 2010 | 2011 | 2012 | 2013 | 2014 | 2015 |
|------|------|------|------|------|------|------|------|------|------|------|
| 4 | 12 | 14 | 9 | 19 | 13 | 14 | 13 | 12 | 15 | 18 |

# Losses

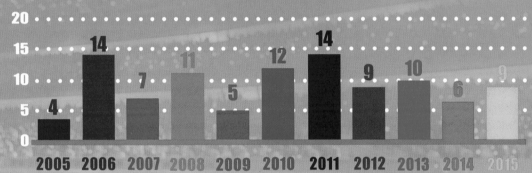

| 2005 | 2006 | 2007 | 2008 | 2009 | 2010 | 2011 | 2012 | 2013 | 2014 | 2015 |
|------|------|------|------|------|------|------|------|------|------|------|
| 4 | 14 | 7 | 11 | 5 | 12 | 14 | 9 | 10 | 6 | 9 |

222
2011

223
2012

216
2013

248
2014

191
2015

25

## Powerful Pitcher

Hernandez has been a star since he was a teen. And he continues to shine. This powerful pitcher has many fans. His fans can't wait to see what he does next.

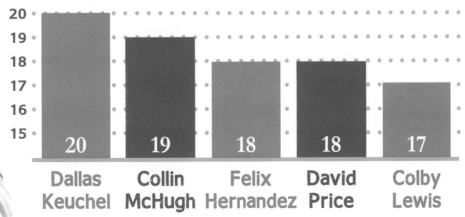

### 2015 American League Pitching Leaders

## Number of Wins

| Dallas Keuchel | Collin McHugh | Felix Hernandez | David Price | Colby Lewis |
|---|---|---|---|---|
| 20 | 19 | 18 | 18 | 17 |

# Timeline

**1986**

**April**

Hernandez is born.

**2002**

**July**

signs with the Mariners

**2003**

**June**

plays first minor league game

**2005**

**August**

plays first major league game

28

**2010**

wins
Cy Young
Award

**2012**

August

pitches
perfect
game

**2014**

July

starts the
All-Star
Game

May

strikes out
2,000th batter
of his MLB
career

**2015**

**inning** (IN-ing)—one of the nine parts of a baseball game in which each team bats until three outs are made

**Latino** (luh-TEE-no)—from Mexico or a country in South America, Central America, or the Caribbean

**loss** (LOHS)—when a baseball pitcher allows a runner to score to take the lead that they never lose

**minor league** (MY-nur LEEG)—a professional baseball organization that competes at levels below the major leagues

**MVP**—an award given to the best player in the league each season; MVP stands for most valuable player.

**scout** (SKOWT)—a person sent to get information about someone or something

**walk** (WAHK)—to go to first base because too many pitches were outside the strike zone

**win** (WIN)—when a baseball player pitches the inning in which the winning team took the lead for the last time

## BOOKS

**Dobrow, Larry.** *Derek Jeter's Ultimate Baseball Guide 2015*. New York: Little Simon, 2015.

**Kelley, K. C.** *Baseball Superstars 2015*. New York: Scholastic Paperback Nonfiction, 2015.

**Stewart, Mark.** *The Seattle Mariners*. Team Spirit. Chicago: Norwood House Press, 2012.

## WEBSITES

Baseball
**www.ducksters.com/sports/baseball.php**

Felix Hernandez
**m.mlb.com/player/433587/felix-hernandez**

Official Seattle Mariners Website
**seattle.mariners.mlb.com**

# INDEX